ONCE UPON A DREAM

Dream A Little Dream

Edited By Briony Kearney

First published in Great Britain in 2024 by:

Young Writers
Remus House
Coltsfoot Drive
Peterborough
PE2 9BF
Telephone: 01733 890066
Website: www.youngwriters.co.uk

All Rights Reserved
Book Design by Ashley Janson
© Copyright Contributors 2024
Softback ISBN 978-1-83685-031-1
Printed and bound in the UK by BookPrintingUK
Website: www.bookprintinguk.com
YB0MA0074A

FOREWORD

Welcome Reader, to a world of dreams.

For Young Writers' latest competition, we asked our writers to dig deep into their imagination and create a poem that paints a picture of what they dream of, whether it's a make-believe world full of wonder or their aspirations for the future.

The result is this collection of fantastic poetic verse that covers a whole host of different topics. Let your mind fly away with the fairies to explore the sweet joy of candy lands, join in with a game of fantasy football, or you may even catch a glimpse of a unicorn or another mythical creature. Beware though, because even dreamland has dark corners, so you may turn a page and walk into a nightmare!

Whereas the majority of our writers chose to stick to a free verse style, others gave themselves the challenge of other techniques such as acrostics and rhyming couplets. We also gave the writers the option to compose their ideas in a story, so watch out for those narrative pieces too!

Each piece in this collection shows the writers' dedication and imagination – we truly believe that seeing their work in print gives them a well-deserved boost of pride, and inspires them to keep writing, so we hope to see more of their work in the future!

CONTENTS

Ashleigh Primary School, Darwen

Lydia Gray (9)	1
Maddison Reid-Knowles (9)	2

Barnsbury Primary School And Nursery, Woking

Isla Beare (8)	3

Bawdeswell Community Primary School, Bawdeswell

Rocco Aldred (10)	4
Violet Aldred (8)	5
Bailey-May Wakes (9)	6

Berrow Primary Church Academy, Berrow

Avin Joseph (11)	7

Betley CE Primary School, Betley

Neave Baldock (10)	8
Jessica Spragg (8)	9
George Batteson (9)	10
Maya Srejic (9)	11
Lottie Edmans (10)	12
Rowen Daly (9)	13

Bryncethin Primary School, Bridgend

Mason Thomas (11)	14

Carterknowle Junior School, Sheffield

Joan Idahosa (7)	15
Hudhayfah Sheraz (8)	16

Cedars Academy, Acocks Green

Saliha Mehmood (10)	17

Cheddar Grove Primary School, Bedminster Down

Muha Nase (10)	18

Ernest Bevin Academy, Tooting

Like Abdur (11)	19
Lewis Chaffey (12)	20
Yousuf Paynda (11)	21
Abdullah Ahamal Din (12)	22

Fairfield Prep School, Loughborough

Raam Patel (10)	23

Fairfields Primary School & Nursery, Flamstead End

Earta Klinaku (11)	24
Berat Coban (9)	25

Folkestone Primary Academy, Folkestone

Atlas Whawhell (8)	26
Miley M (7)	27

Frederick Bird Primary School, Coventry

Sentia Kutubali (10)	28

Goonhavern Primary School, Goonhavern

Oren Montgomery (10)	29
Albert P (10)	30

Grange Farm Primary School, Leeds

Magdiel Kyeremeh (10)	31
Raven Diamond (9)	32

Gurney Pease Academy, Darlington

Margaret-Rose Ward (10)	33
Wayne Johnson (9)	34

Hesketh-With-Becconsall All Saints CE School, Hesketh Bank

Abbie Tree (8)	35
Jonah Kitchen (8)	36

Highcliffe Primary School, Birstall

Sienna Desousa (8)	37

Hill Top CE Primary School, Low Moor

Logan Moore (9)	39
Dominik Gasion (8)	40
Oliver Gonsalkrorale (9)	41
Keiron Pattison (9)	42

Jorge Day (9)	43

Hillside Avenue Primary And Nursery School, Norwich

Bonnie Bello (9)	44

Holy Trinity Primary School, Waltham Cross

Josiah Curtis-Broni (7)	45
Yedaiah Adu Gyamfi (7)	46

Khalsa (VA) Primary School, Southall

Maanya Kaur Soni (8)	47
Gurleen Kaur Aujla (10)	48
Anoopjot Singh (8)	49
Ersheen Kaur (9)	50

King David Primary School, Crumpsall

Tallulah Abelson (10)	51
Isabella Swerdlow (9)	52
Annabelle Benjamin (10)	53
Oscar Marks (10)	54
Jamie Serene (9)	55
Yoni Goldman (10)	56

Kingsway Junior School, Watford

Maisie Rolls (7)	57

Little Chalfont Primary School, Little Chalfont

Charlotte Brier (8)	58
Aarav Mody (9)	59
Anaya Mody (9)	60

Loders Primary Academy, Loders

Rosie Way (9)	61
Toby Webster (8)	62

Long Crendon School, Long Crendon

Gwyn Thomas (10)	63

Lote Tree Primary School, Foleshill

Ibraheem Rafiq (10)	64

Maple Grove Primary School, Pitsea

Abdullah Jamal (8)	65
Ria Kandola (9)	66

Meadow Primary School, Stoneleigh

Rishi Shah (10)	67

Meanwood Primary School, Rochdale

Falak Waqas (10)	68

Meole Brace Church Of England Primary And Nursery, Shrewsbury

Sarah Taylor (9)	69

Merton Junior School, Basingstoke

Idiatou Bahri (9)	71

Moorlands Junior School, Sale

Maryam Kazmi (7)	72

North Town Primary School, Taunton

Byron Cusack-Atkinson	73

Northwood College For Girls (GDST), Northwood

Navya Malani (8)	74
Tvisha Patel (9)	75
Mia Onwugbonu (10)	76
Shagun Patel (9)	77
Darcey Brown (9)	78
Krupali Patel (9)	79

Notting Hill Preparatory School, London

Billy Sharples (12)	80
Rufus Hult (12)	81
Electra Michalopoulou (11)	82

Oakwood Junior School, Derby

Annas Ahmadi (8)	83

Offley Primary Academy, Sandbach

Harry Astles (10)	84

Oldbury Park Primary School, Worcester

Jack Strain (9)	85

Pencombe CE Primary School, Pencombe

Kacper Aniolek (8)	86

Reddal Hill Primary School, Cradley Heath

Mehek Iman (10)	87

Rishworth School, Rishworth

Harriet Dangerfield (8)	88

River Mill Primary School, Dartford

Gabriella Enemuwe (8)	89

Rydes Hill Preparatory School, Guildford

Kiana Allaraj (9)	90
Arya Srivastava (9)	91
Ajaalet Breen (9)	92
Myra Srivastava (9)	93

Sacred Heart Catholic Primary School, Middlesbrough

Ruth Kidane (8)	94
Jude Weedon (9)	95

St Anne's RC Primary School, Lambeth

Luana Silveira (9)	96
Pema Chilanga-Halbritter (9)	97
Valentina Mora (9)	98
Armani Taffe (9)	99

St Colmcille's Primary School, Carrickmore

Mattie McCallan (10)	100
Ryan Loughran (10)	102
Eoghan Donnelly (11)	103

St Edward's CE Primary School, Castleton

Isabelle Mcleannan Greaves (9)	104
Isabella Arrowsmith (10)	105
Aizah Khan (10)	106

St Joseph's Catholic Primary School, Newbury

Jayden Wills (9)	107
Ishaan Sai Prasanna (9)	108

St Mary's Catholic Primary School, Canton

Melia Payne (9)	109
Naomi Solomon (9)	110
Joel Eze (9)	112

St Matthew's Church Of England Primary School, Redhill

Jessica Gerrie (8)	113
Gracielle Romero (7)	114

St Meryl School, Watford

Richard Buzenschi (10)	115
Indi Horwood (10)	116
Louis F (10)	117
Ruth Prelipcean (10)	118

St Michael's CE Primary School, Braintree

Esmay Bou-Yeldham	119

St Patrick's Catholic Primary School, Leeds

Charlotte Dixon (10)	121
Adaeze Anyawueze (10)	122

St Pius X Catholic Preparatory School, Fulwood

Hasnain Bhatia (8)	123
Tinaye Mleng (9)	124

Stanborough Primary School, Garston

Hana Swain (9)	125
Fatima Moshen (8)	126
Ved Patel (9)	127

Sutterton Fourfields CE Primary School, Sutterton

Alexander Wilson-Reeves (8)	128
Mollie Quincey (8)	129

The King's School, Gloucester

Sebastian Williams (10)	130
Pippa Hay (10)	131

The Oval Primary School, Birmingham

Lima Sadyar (8)	132
Lubna Hatif (8)	133
Binyamin Shah (9)	134
Fatima Latif (9)	135
Anayah Bibi (9)	136
Maya Anasiasta (9)	137
Aila Hussain (8)	138
Mohammed Hassan (9)	139
Umaima Asim (8)	140
Aiza Hussain (8)	141
Aisha Ali (9)	142
Safiyyah Islam (9)	143
Muhammad Zubair (9)	144

The Ridgeway Primary School, Reading

Tianna-Mai Jones (10)	145

Towers Junior School, Hornchurch

Janiah Katenda (7)	146
Kyra Sains (10)	148
George Rayner (11)	149

Trawden Forest Primary School, Trawden

Cassius Castro (9)	150

Wembdon St George's CE VC Primary School, Wembdon

Isla Rossiter (9)	151
Indie Rogers (10)	152

Whetstone Field Primary School, Walsall

Sofia Ishaq (9)	153
Ivy Wilkes (9)	154
Pratik Shah (8)	155
Fearne Karim (9)	156
Freddy Montgomery (8)	157
Ollie Whiting (9)	158

THE CREATIVE WRITING

The Mythical War

In Neverland, the skies were pink, the clouds were purple. Everywhere was calm 'til the nasty candy pirates came. There were eighty candy pirates and then in one week it all changed. It was eighty warrior fairies against five candy pirates. But the only reason they were winning was because they ate snozberries and bunny poo (ew!).
And then the world's best person came, Ronaldo and he was shouting *suii* but no one knew what time it was because it was seven o'clock all the time.

Lydia Gray (9)
Ashleigh Primary School, Darwen

Once Upon A Dream

Some birds were rolling on the ground
The tree waved at his friend
With his blue-leafed arms
The flower is buzzing and the bee smells sweet
They are going on the school bus to school to learn
Their packed lunches on their knees
Pigs are busy cleaning their rooms
And the sheep are washing the dishes.

Maddison Reid-Knowles (9)
Ashleigh Primary School, Darwen

The Northern Lights

The Northern Lights
You shine so bright
On this clear and starry night
Your colours gleam
And your colours stream
Through my whole and beating heart.

Isla Beare (8)
Barnsbury Primary School And Nursery, Woking

My Dreamland...

Flying, smiley faces as fast as an Olympic athlete
Talking clocks that tell the time, any time
Jub-Jub birds as hungry as a ravenous human
Dancing pigs as happy as a hyperactive toddler
Baked beans falling from the sky like rain
Crocodiles parachuting like hailstones falling onto pavement
As white, freshly-made cream aliens fly around in UFOs as fast as a car.

Rocco Aldred (10)
Bawdeswell Community Primary School, Bawdeswell

Candy Land

A land that's made of colourful candy,
The clouds are made of cotton candy,
Floats sweetly across the land,
The Matchmaker trees stand straight and tall,
Guarding the chocolate wall,
The flowers are made of Jelly Tots,
The river flows like hot chocolate.

Violet Aldred (8)
Bawdeswell Community Primary School, Bawdeswell

Secret Dream Land

You will see bouncing unicorns on rainbows, floating in a magical wild dream. Everyone's welcome with bouncing flowers and chatty teapots waving and floating on top of rainbow clouds in the sky.

Bailey-May Wakes (9)
Bawdeswell Community Primary School, Bawdeswell

Dream Of Magic World

I saw Owen playing football and he scored fifteen goals and Milo scored ten goals. Then Owen and Milo played Fortnite and Owen won.
They both went to Oscar's house and their football went pop and they seemed sad. The three went sadly to their homes and went to sleep.
It became morning. The three went to school and Owen and Milo met each other and they played.

Avin Joseph (11)
Berrow Primary Church Academy, Berrow

Lost In A Dream...

I was at a normal concert,
When I thought I needed comfort,
Then I turned around and all my family had gone,
But when I leaned back, I started getting trodden on,
And when I realised I was lost,
Suddenly, I saw some frost,
Then everyone leaves,
And I had fallen to my knees,
When I started to cry, I grew terrified,
As I heard someone who sighed,
And then they took me away,
But it turned out I wanted to stay,
Thankfully, I woke up,
And I was right next to the pup.

Neave Baldock (10)
Betley CE Primary School, Betley

I Want To Be A Footballer

I want to be a footballer, so I can score a goal,
But if I kick the ball too far, it might go to the North Pole.

I'll play midfield on the left wing,
It's so exciting, I feel like I could sing.

I'll play for Liverpool Ladies because that's the team I love so much,
But if I get an injury, I might be on a crutch.

I want to be a footballer when I grow up,
I hope I don't have to wait much longer because I want to win that cup.

Jessica Spragg (8)
Betley CE Primary School, Betley

I Fly To The Milky Way

I am living on the sun as normal,
When a flying dinosaur appears in front of me.
I hop aboard the dinosaur and fly to the Milky Way.

This is who I want to be,
As we just met.
We should have a banquet,
As we just met.

I fly to the Milky Way,
For my first day.
I am over the moon,
I feel like a spoon.

Flying on a dinosaur,
It is a very weird feeling.
When we go through the portal,
As I fly to the Milky Way.

George Batteson (9)
Betley CE Primary School, Betley

Dreamland

Candy Dreamland, it's like a dream.
Rising up like a sunlight beam.
Coming near, coming down.
Coming here with a big brown frown.
Comes a pet called Mandy,
Stuck to lots of candy.
Puts out a paw, very sticky.
Better not touch, it'll be icky.
There's lots of blooms,
But also spoons.
I wave goodbye,
And look up at the sky.
I'll miss this place,
But I have to go to my own race.

Maya Srejic (9)
Betley CE Primary School, Betley

Wonderland

This land of wonder was odd and off,
As there were cows that could fly
And fairies that danced
And the clouds were pink.
As I entered a house of candy and cake,
The cake was good, but I got told off.

Lottie Edmans (10)
Betley CE Primary School, Betley

A Dark Dream

D ark mist surrounds me
R eminding me of bad memories
E ntering a dark tunnel
A machine sucks me in
M y dream is over. I'm home again.

Rowen Daly (9)
Betley CE Primary School, Betley

Untitled

I dreamed a dream,
Of a world of beauty.

I dreamed a dream,
Of a world of no crimes.

I dreamed a dream,
Of a world of no wars.

I dreamed a dream,
Of a world of no hunger.

I dreamed a dream,
Of a world of no pollution.

I dreamed a dream,
Of a world with no dirty water.

Mason Thomas (11)
Bryncethin Primary School, Bridgend

My Unicorn

She stands so still and alert
Her head is cocked to hear
Her delicate nostrils flare about her
The snow looks like dirt.

She blows out soft, warm breath
Her horn is so beautiful
Nothing about her is dull
She lowers her great white head
Her eyes are wide and full of trust.

She looks as though she smiles
With a face as full of content as a young child
She glorifies even the surrounding dust.

Joan Idahosa (7)
Carterknowle Junior School, Sheffield

God Is Cool

God is cool
God looks cool
God is the best in the whole, entire universe.

Hudhayfah Sheraz (8)
Carterknowle Junior School, Sheffield

Past Till Now

Yardley was once a quiet area,
Say the people from the early 2000s,
Now it is overcrowded,
Say the cars that are roaring down the road.
Yardley was once just homes,
Say its constructors,
Now it is a place of business,
Say the shops that are lying on the ground.
Yardley was a new place,
Says the last century,
Now it is old,
Say the people from the 2000s.
Yardley was an ecstatic place,
Now it is old,
But Yardley is the best at keeping memories,
Says me.

Saliha Mehmood (10)
Cedars Academy, Acocks Green

The Real World...

Poems for Palestine
There is more spilled blood than drinkable water in Gaza
Off the news the kids are crying, hide them away
Comfort them with lies
Dreams shattered by missiles' might
A community in need, fading from sight
Gaze through the window, children run and play
Is it a game of tag or danger in their way?

People play and laugh, run and dance
But sometimes I just feel left out
"Wow, she is so pretty," and then I look at myself
I say to myself, "Come on, Muha, you're strong, smart, kind, you're funny
Just smile and if someone is reading this, you are not alone
Just smile because you are my little star!"

Muha Nase (10)
Cheddar Grove Primary School, Bedminster Down

I Dream Of Being A Pirate

Being a pirate
Is the best, sailing
Across the sea,
Exploring the world
And places.

Treasure chests
Are waiting
To be opened. There are
Other pirates who
Try to take our
Territory, so we
Make a truce.

When a truce is
Made, flintlocks
Aren't locked
And loaded. There
Is a journey to
Be continued.

Like Abdur (11)
Ernest Bevin Academy, Tooting

Exploring

The world is a playground,
Go out on foot, a car, a train, a plane,
The world is so large, so much to explore,
Travel on a brown boat to the land of dreams,
Take a rocket into the galaxy or
A submarine deep into an unexplored trench,
The list goes on,
Go out and do a little bit of exploring.

Lewis Chaffey (12)
Ernest Bevin Academy, Tooting

Is It A Dream?

Flying through the sky,
Is it a dream?
Fighting monsters,
Is it a dream?
First person to land on Mars,
Is it a dream?
Walking on the red carpet,
Is it a dream?
Finally getting your favourite game,
Is it a dream?
Waking up,
Is it a dream?

Yousuf Paynda (11)
Ernest Bevin Academy, Tooting

Famous And Rich

I want to be rich and famous
I want to buy cars
I want to touch the sky
I would have wings on my shoulders
I would get the respect without being nice
Never be in the darkness
Living in the light
No blindfold on my eyes
Knowing the real people.

Abdullah Ahamal Din (12)
Ernest Bevin Academy, Tooting

Flying Through The Starry Sky

I'm riding through the starry sky with an owl by my side
We start to swiftly float and glide
As we fly through the night sky
We can touch and scoop the clouds up high.

We are quicker than an antelope
And we can even see further than a telescope
As we slowly begin our descend
I feel like we are going to a dead-end.

Suddenly, we've crashed
We're trapped
I woke up with dread
But soon realised I was safe tucked up in bed.

Raam Patel (10)
Fairfield Prep School, Loughborough

Nightmare

In my nightmare, I saw a big dangerous clown haunting me.
As I was walking through a cornfield, I heard the wind howling for the darkness to spread.
As I walked further and further, I stepped on a small oval mirror. When I looked in the mirror I saw a creepy clown face. My heart was beating very fast.
I looked quickly behind and saw nothing.
As I was walking, I spotted a big poster of a clown. I got very worried.
As I went through the cornfield I saw red, gleaming eyes looking at me angrily.
It came closer and closer and then I saw the creepy clown that I had seen in the mirror.
I started running as fast as I could because I didn't want to get eaten by the clown.
Then soon I woke up in my bed. I was so happy that it was just a dream and not real.

Earta Klinaku (11)
Fairfields Primary School & Nursery, Flamstead End

YouTuber

My dream is to be a YouTuber to create good videos. I love doing prank video games and shorts to get lots of views. And do fireworks when I get ten million followers. The gold plaque and silver plaque.

Berat Coban (9)
Fairfields Primary School & Nursery, Flamstead End

The Challenge I Won

In my dreams each night,
I go to amazing California on a flight,
Every time I hope to fulfil my dream,
With all that money I could make a stream,
Once I arrived in California,
I really do have to warn ya,
It is so warm there, I stayed inside,
My sister, however, was filled with pride,
Once I met up with MrBeast,
He invited me over to have a feast,
Then we set up the challenge,
One of the obstacles made a hot dog singer,
First, someone called Neal went,
Surely enough he was from Kent,
I ended up winning because I had the faster times,
And MrBeast paid me all in dimes!

Atlas Whawhell (8)
Folkestone Primary Academy, Folkestone

Dreams

D ancing with dogs
R ed roses walking everywhere
E lephants swimming in the pool
A mazing animals playing in the park
M agic monkeys sit in my mind
S illy snakes crawling everywhere.

Miley M (7)
Folkestone Primary Academy, Folkestone

The Magical Dream

Me and my best friend,
In the park,
At midnight sky,
With stars sparkling, with light on every one of them,
As we watch the beauty of the midnight sky,
We see something mythical,
We use our powers, and fly through the midnight sky,
We find the creature,
With fairy-like wings and blue, sparkling eyes, flying in the midnight sky,
Me and my best friend approach this mythical creature,
And find out it is a fairy,
We play with the fairy, as we watch the beauty of the midnight sky,
With sparkling stars and light on every one of them,
Waking up to the sun,
And finding out,
That it was all just a magical dream.

Sentia Kutubali (10)
Frederick Bird Primary School, Coventry

Jeff's Death

J effry is cool
E ats a lot of breakfast
F ood is nice
F ood like mine
S uper Jeff

D oom will come
E ndless torture
A nd it will never stop
T he pain
H urts, it's death.

Oren Montgomery (10)
Goonhavern Primary School, Goonhavern

Breathtaking View
A haiku

Beautiful all round
Dreamy, natural beauty
Unbelievable.

Albert P (10)
Goonhavern Primary School, Goonhavern

Nightmare Of Doom

N ights are for sleeping. Right? But why do we sleep?
I don't know, is it to experience dreams that leap?
G reat, just hope you don't have a nightmare
H ey, you are in a nightmare, don't worry, it's just a nightmare
T ake a deep breath. As you are breathing, a dream
M ay try to gleam, at least be gleamy
A rgh, oh no, black is all you see
R un, you are at sea
E ek, we are your worst nightmare

O h, sleepy, don't wake up till the morning
F ine, face the truth but don't be moaning

D one, no time to think and just stay in a moment
O h, are we in the moment?
O oh, nightmare of doom
M ay look to the moon but don't forget dreams fly through our imagination. The happier the imagination, the less chance of a nightmare.

Magdiel Kyeremeh (10)
Grange Farm Primary School, Leeds

Nightmares Of Doom

N othing has prepared me for the thing I see.
I took a step forward, as scared as can be.
G lancing left and right, all I see is flames.
H ow did I get here? I hope to find out their names.
T hud! Thud! Something moved - it's creeping up.
M y worst nightmare has come true. It's a Monster Moo.
A scary grin spread around its face.
R unning like a squirrel, it starts to chase.
E very eye began to glow. I close my own in dread.
S uddenly, I wake up to find myself in my bed!

O verall, I decided to stay in my bed.
"F ollow me," someone said, as I realised I hit my head.

"D on't leave," it said to me.
O verall, I said to it to leave me be.
"O h no!" I said after I heard a scream.
M y head woke me up after the dream.

Raven Diamond (9)
Grange Farm Primary School, Leeds

Raging Nightmares

R unning through the forest, my feet choose to slip
A round me, creatures roam like an ant on a stick
G rowling runs around me. Shall I run or shall I lay
I n my head I'm wondering will this be my last day
N o way, I will stay laying
"**G** o, start running," the voices are saying

N *ever stop*, I say in my head
I n that moment, my legs get tired and I'm full of dread
G iant tears drop down my eyes
H ow is this not the day I die?
T oo many creatures are around me now
M y body is like a river in a lion crowd
A rrangements look like they're being made
R esting my head I lie behind a log
E very monster circles me and begins to hog
S omething tells me death is soon. Goodbye world, I'm leaving you.

Margaret-Rose Ward (10)
Gurney Pease Academy, Darlington

Dream

D inosaurs are cool
R oyalty is special
E ating is not good
A thletes do exercise
M onsters are scary.

Wayne Johnson (9)
Gurney Pease Academy, Darlington

Over The Stars

O ver the rooftops, as high as the stars,
V ery tender, it is all ours,
E very sparkle, shimmer or light,
R ecommended, oh, so very bright.

T he wish that I can't get out,
H ave a big flap about,
E very star is worth a royalty.

S uddenly, I was back home,
T he world, all like a dome,
A little thought popped into my head,
R eplaced and tucked into bed,
S o much to think about.

Abbie Tree (8)
Hesketh-With-Becconsall All Saints CE School, Hesketh Bank

Once, I Had A Dream

I was in a fight with
A big poisonous dragon

With my friends, Juxon and William,
We defeated the beast

Once I had a dream
I was in a bright green field
Trying to escape a
Big, black and red giant with my friends
We got him on the floor and that
Gave us time to escape to an abandoned motel
And drive away.

Jonah Kitchen (8)
Hesketh-With-Becconsall All Saints CE School, Hesketh Bank

Spider Land!

Up in the clouds, way up high,
there is a majestic portal in the sky.
The portal was leading to another dimension,
so I went in!
I went in the swirling portal,
knowing I had no idea where I was going!
I landed on the ground with a thump!
Then I looked head to back
and soon I realised I had a pack.
I opened the pack with such confusion,
I looked inside and I thought
my mind was going crazy like an illusion!
Inside the pack was my very own spider!
I happily took my friend and played
on the slide, merry-go-round and swing!
I soon realised I was in Spider Land!
Spider Land is a place of memories
that you would keep forever!
As me and my little friends waited for the movie,
I got two tickets and that meant
I got free popcorn!
Then it was time to go and watch the movie!

After the movie, I said goodbye
and went back into the portal way up high
in the sky.

Sienna Desousa (8)
Highcliffe Primary School, Birstall

Carnivores

As flowers bloomed in the darkness of the forest, as people and animals sprinted through the forest of the wilds, as a person walked by and inspected a tree, a giant pack of leopards and lions all walked together to take down three humans.

Five snow leopards, three speedy leopards, nine jaguars, two black panthers and two female and male lions all attacked.

The birds swooped down to kill the carnivores. The birds were defending the humans, but twenty-seven birds weren't enough to take on so many carnivores. Only two of them survived, but one of them had superpowers of healing. He healed the other and they escaped.

Logan Moore (9)
Hill Top CE Primary School, Low Moor

Space Football

S oon I went to space
P eople screaming for the win
A lot of people chanting in the crowd
C ould that please be a penalty?
E veryone screaming along.

F oot on the ball taking the penalty
O h no, he missed the best shot
O ther people said that it was in
T ake the kick-off, it was a goal
B all immediately took an age
A million fans want a goal
L lamas suddenly come on the pitch
L osers, losers, our team won.

Dominik Gasion (8)
Hill Top CE Primary School, Low Moor

Rainforest

R ight in the middle of the rainforest
A great big fire lion as light as the sun
I n the jar also great snakes lie as
N ear to us as a hat that gets blown off by a
F urious gust of wind. Parrots fly
O ver our heads as quick as a cheetah
R ustling in the wind the bushes shout
E ndlessly I walk along the path
S uddenly a roar as loud as the fire lion but
T hen I suddenly wake up snug in my bed.

Oliver Gonsalkrorale (9)
Hill Top CE Primary School, Low Moor

Football

F ootsteps outside
O n the shed was a person who was wearing an
O range jacket, he was laughing at me. He went
T o the door and knocked loudly, bang! I opened the door
B ang, bang! Again I checked the back door
A nd the man was running, I chased him for a
L ong time, he got tired so I caught him. My
L egs were tired, but I pushed through it all and then I saw him, it was a pirate flying a long way.

Keiron Pattison (9)
Hill Top CE Primary School, Low Moor

Dream Jungle

On a gloomy and stormy night, I woke up to find a jungle infested with flying stingrays in the gloomy jungle and one of the flying stingrays flew me to the moon but my mum shouted at me. It was all a dream.

Jorge Day (9)
Hill Top CE Primary School, Low Moor

The Star Fairy

The star fairy
shining bright
taking light
from the night.
A tiny little fairy, all alone
trying to do big things in a lonely tone.
But a star came passing by
and she was so shy.
But she took what it takes
and their hands were starting to shake.
I hope you like this poem
and tell your friends
or show them.

Bonnie Bello (9)
Hillside Avenue Primary And Nursery School, Norwich

Once Upon A Dream

G etting lost with my brother, nowhere to go
E aten by a bear
T ime to camp
T oo late! He eats us
I nside of the bear was flesh
N asty smells
G rizzly teeth

L astly, we get out of the bear
O h! Yay! The bear is gone!
S et the tent up, I will get food
T ime to go to sleep - goodnight.

Josiah Curtis-Broni (7)
Holy Trinity Primary School, Waltham Cross

Untitled

H elicopters in the sky,
U nder beds creatures fly,
N o electricity in the kitchen,
T oo many eating chicken,
E very room empty,
D ogs eat me.

Yedaiah Adu Gyamfi (7)
Holy Trinity Primary School, Waltham Cross

Crazy Miss Little Unicorn

"Look at me
I can sing
I can dance and
I can fly
With bright colours in the sky."
They are kind
They are brave
They are unique.
They always wake up tired and lazy like a slow snail.
Such dirty unicorns because they never take a shower.
They have dirty ears and never cut their nails.
They always fight with lions for no reason.
A unicorn lived over a rainbow with friends.
They always have pretty colours and magical horns.
They want to follow me all the time.
They always give their powers to people
Like they don't know what they are doing.
They always eat junk food
They always drink fizzy drinks.

Maanya Kaur Soni (8)
Khalsa (VA) Primary School, Southall

My Dreams

M ystical creatures in an enchanted forest
Y et to realise that

D eep down in the forest, a witch is
R eady to pounce.
E arly the next morning, all unicorns, dragons get ready for this
A ttack.
M oments later, the terrifying woman came.
S he never expected this.

In seconds, she was defeated and the mystic creatures were yet again free.

Gurleen Kaur Aujla (10)
Khalsa (VA) Primary School, Southall

The Footballers

Footballers wandering around the pitch
Scoring goals and smashing goals
Often, fans scream and shout when their favourite team scores
Come on, Man City, you can do it!
We have Gündoğan in midfield
And Haaland in forward
Arsenal lost 3-1 to Man City
Come on, Man City, you can *do it!*

Anoopjot Singh (8)
Khalsa (VA) Primary School, Southall

A Famous Girl

A girl is famous

But is nameless
Did not win a scholarship
Because she is brainless

Her place is spacious
Also, she blamed us.

Ersheen Kaur (9)
Khalsa (VA) Primary School, Southall

A Beauty-ful Dream

When I think about the amazing things I would like to be
I dream up and imagine the creative things for you all to see
From beauty and skincare, a facialist too
Or maybe a hairdresser with a view to help you
I know that if I think of these things I could be
My mum, especially, would be proud of me
Or maybe I could work as an artist or a buyer
You see, the list is endless if you only set your sights higher
Maybe I'll be famous with a make-up line
A beauty ambassador but these things take time
Creating my own skincare brand, now that's a dream
Or maybe some make-up or beauty cream
But one thing I know, whatever will be
Being happy and successful is key.

Tallulah Abelson (10)
King David Primary School, Crumpsall

The Fantastic Goal Of Jack Grealish

Grealish kicked the ball so high
It gave him magic powers and made him fly
He landed in outer space
He met an astronaut who asked him for a race
The astronaut happened to be me
Jack agreed to race with me happily
We ran so fast
A spaceship zoomed past
All of a sudden, we were lost, this made us sad
How would we make it back to the Etihad?
Jack used his powers to contact the team
Was this real or was this a dream?
Next thing I knew, Jack and I were on the sideline
Pep asked me if I would like to play after half-time
I scored a goal on my debut.

Isabella Swerdlow (9)
King David Primary School, Crumpsall

In The Act

My eyes shut tight
As I slip into the night
Dancing, prancing, hurling
Visiting places that are concerning
How I want to join the act

There I am happy as can be
I've climbed up high for all to see
Front of stage applause is great
Even me, I can relate
How I want to join the act

Think I'm famous, lights on me
Dressed so fancy, everyone can see
Flickering phones don't blind me
I'm so happy that all can see
Now I am... in the act.

Annabelle Benjamin (10)
King David Primary School, Crumpsall

Golf Life

On Augusta's green so grand
Oscar Marks makes his stand
Tiger Woods, a legend tall
Fell to Oscar's perfect fall

With steady hand and iron will
Oscar climbed the fabled hill
A birdie putt, a victory clear
Echoed through the Master's cheer

In annals, bold and bright
Oscar Marks' triumphant night.

Oscar Marks (10)
King David Primary School, Crumpsall

The Winning Match

Football, oh football, my dream of football
How quite nice it is to play some football
The crowds are cheering so loudly
It's making me feel so proud
My teammate kicks the ball to me
I run along, feeling so happy
Finally, it's my chance
I score and dance.

Jamie Serene (9)
King David Primary School, Crumpsall

Untitled

I was with my brother once in my garden
I had a bargain with a footballer
He got lost, so I showed him the way
So, I told him the way back home and he said, "Hooray!"
The moral of this poem is, never choose a role model over yourself and your family.

Yoni Goldman (10)
King David Primary School, Crumpsall

The Treasure

In my dream, I walked through a beautiful park. Suddenly, we heard a loud neigh. A bright shimmering unicorn popped up. Me and my friend looked at each other in fear. The peach unicorn bowed her head. She said, "Come with me." We nodded at each other and jumped on her back. She took us to a white, pretty tree. We climbed to the top, as high as the sky. She nodded her head to show us a glowing hole. We looked inside with glee. It was full of precious jewellery and gold.

Maisie Rolls (7)
Kingsway Junior School, Watford

Nightmares To Dreams

There were falling holes, talking moles,
And monsters roaming in and out,
While witches cast their spells about,
But fairies came,
So happiness did the same,
So kindness spread,
Monsters dread,
The worst thing that would be
Would be monsters being
Happy or having to flee.

Charlotte Brier (8)
Little Chalfont Primary School, Little Chalfont

The Unfortunate Cricket Ball

There was once an old cricket ball,
That was bought from a shopping mall,
The partner, the bat,
Who was very fat,
Which gave him the worst life of all.

Aarav Mody (9)
Little Chalfont Primary School, Little Chalfont

Candyland

There was once a gingerbread man,
Who lived in a Candyland,
There were candyfloss clouds,
And lots of clouds,
Once in a Candyland.

Anaya Mody (9)
Little Chalfont Primary School, Little Chalfont

The Race

I'm on the racetrack, ready to race
I can match Mario's pace
I'm the fastest in the land
I even have a cool rubber band
I look at the line and it's time to go
To an interview, no time to change, just wait a mo
But the boss is a cat, but talking
And a talking dog.

Rosie Way (9)
Loders Primary Academy, Loders

Dragons

I drifted off into a deep sleep,
Before my eyes, dragons roam in sight,
Dragons everywhere, green, red, purple,
All coloured, grey, black,
Old, mossy castle with treasure for years,
It's lonely and scary with dragons.

Toby Webster (8)
Loders Primary Academy, Loders

The Difference In Nightmares And Dreams

Dreams can be anything, anything at all,
Maybe you'll meet a man who's very tall,
Or maybe you'll fly very high in the sky,
Nothing is normal, trust me now,
You could make friends with a talking cow,
Maybe you'll find a rainbow cat,
Or you'll meet an acrobat.

Sometimes, you'll have nightmares,
That aren't very nice,
Maybe you'll get eaten by giant mice,
But all you need to remember is they aren't true,
So, just open your eyes and enjoy
Being you!

Gwyn Thomas (10)
Long Crendon School, Long Crendon

Vampires

V ampires, venomous vampires everywhere
A vampire here and there
M iniature ones, huge ones, I cry in my bed
P eter wishes he was dead
I 'm locked in my house night and day
R uthless maniacs in my head
E erie faces I still remember
S aid I'm sorry for what I did.

Ibraheem Rafiq (10)
Lote Tree Primary School, Foleshill

The Fairy World

Once upon a time, there was a boy called Daniel. One sunny day, Daniel was walking in the jungle. Suddenly, he saw a beautiful fairy world. He was shocked because he was in the jungle.

He entered the beautiful fairy world. He was shocked because the palace was in the sky - everything was in the sky. He needed to go up the stairs to get into the beautiful fairy world.

When he went in, the fairies took him to the palace. When he saw it, he liked the palace because it had butterflies in it.

Abdullah Jamal (8)
Maple Grove Primary School, Pitsea

The Magic Forest

As the moon shines in the midnight sky,
I follow the glowing mushrooms,
To see where I go.

Oh, if I knew what was in this majestic forest,
In the distance, owls are hooting and moving,
While I wander and wander...

Suddenly, I see a shine,
A shine so bright, I can barely see!
And to my surprise, standing there is a unicorn with a ruby mane!

Ria Kandola (9)
Maple Grove Primary School, Pitsea

Stars

When the sky is dark and day turns to night,
Out come the stars and they glow very bright,
They twinkle here and they twinkle there,
Making constellations like a bear.

I see them every night, when the sun is at rest,
And that is when I see them, the very best,
A twinkle here and a twinkle there,
They are almost everywhere!

With a trail of light, a shooting star passes by,
Then another one comes up but it starts to die,
Leaving a mysterious trail behind it,
Yet I still wonder what it is like to be a star.

Rishi Shah (10)
Meadow Primary School, Stoneleigh

The Monster Undersea

Every night, every day,
I look outside from the bay,
In the sea, I see a hand,
My feet under the sand,
I dive into the ocean and look around,
But all there is, is a quiet sound,
I panic and try to go back to shore,
But now I hear a dangerous roar,
I look around,
And it continues to make that sound,
Then something pushes me towards the beach,
And it gives me a little screech,
Then I see its limb,
It was actually a human hand!

Falak Waqas (10)
Meanwood Primary School, Rochdale

Going In Wonderland

Beautiful, pretty flowers,
A tea party with a person
As mad as a goose
With a hat and an umbrella.

I'm with my friend Snowy,
Her hair is as black as darkness,
She is kind,
Nice and helpful.

I'm in Wonderland,
Trees as big as a boulder,
The flowers are crying
As they get stepped on.

I feel like a cloud,
As light as a feather,
I feel happy
And joyful with Snowy.

I have a tea party
With Snowy, we met
A cat that is pink
And purple, he has a big smile.

We had to run
As fast as we could
Because the queen
Was going to chop our heads.

We ran and escaped
But we were lost
We nearly got out
But it cost!

Sarah Taylor (9)
Meole Brace Church Of England Primary And Nursery, Shrewsbury

Enchanted Forest

E ven I don't know where I am. I can't see
N othing except as I open my eyes, the sun is
C hanting my name. I have never seen a strange thing in my life
H owever, an unfamiliar thing ran through the darkness
A figure that I have never seen before
N o, it was something I couldn't quite see
T hen it came closer and then I moved in
E ven though I
D idn't believe it

F or a second, my mind went blank
O r I actually saw the endangered unicorns. I was
R ight but it was injured on its left leg
E ven though I felt bad it was still
S cared. I helped her and took her
T o safety.

Idiatou Bahri (9)
Merton Junior School, Basingstoke

Heavenly Place

The cute, friendly dinosaurs are as adorable as kittens,
The penguins are wearing cute knitted mittens.

The elegant baby cheetahs roam around the land,
The little red crabs are crawling around the sand.

In this world, we make potions to keep ourselves magical,
In this world, we wear lotion to keep ourselves funny.

I have a pet called Sara and she is a farmer,
I have a pet named Liana the llama.

Tomorrow, I will go on a hike,
Back in the day, I rode on my bike.

I am at the fair and I am having fun,
I am in space and I am exploring the sun.

Maryam Kazmi (7)
Moorlands Junior School, Sale

The Space Pirate Dream

When I drift off to sleep, the world of dreams is released. With a crash and a thud, I awoke with a bang but I did not care a hang. I flounced and I pounced up into the open air it was a party m'harty, a celebration, a brew, but who in the world would have a party at half past two? I had to run, I had to whip through just to find out actually who, but then, just then, I realised now I was on a pirate's vessel.

Byron Cusack-Atkinson
North Town Primary School, Taunton

My Dream...

My dream is to be an artist
An artist who loves nature
An artist who loves colours.
In my dream, I am in my art world full of nature
And lots and lots and lots of colours like
Red, orange, yellow, green, blue, purple, pink, etc.
I live in a mansion like a princess
I have a beautiful bedroom with everything you could possibly whisper.
At lunch and dinner, I can have whatever food I want.
That mansion is like the best place in the world
Well, because it is my dreamland.
After breakfast, I go to my magic portal
And after you go there, there is a classroom at 9:00
I have lessons where I teach people, art of course
Because, like, it's my favourite subject
And it's the best subject ever
Well, I better end it there
Hope you have a very nice day
Bye, bye, see you later.

Navya Malani (8)
Northwood College For Girls (GDST), Northwood

Floating On A Cloud

F lowers dance joyfully around me
L ittle bunnies hopping around excitedly
O ver the field, I float
A round the meadow, I drift with the morning breeze
T rifles, cupcakes and candy galore
I reach out for one, it melts as it touches my fingers
N ot a miserable person in sight
G reen luscious grass sways peacefully

O n and on I float, drifting further into the distance
N o one can ruin the moment for me

A s if it was trained, a fluffy bunny jumps into my arms

C louds made of cotton candy
L ove and joy fill the air
O nce upon a dream...
U nderneath me, a meadow filled with colourful flowers
D ear little rabbits pop out to say hi.

Tvisha Patel (9)
Northwood College For Girls (GDST), Northwood

Candy Queen

C an you ever feel the joy when you eat
A lmond joy fills you with energy
N utritious foods are no better than candy
D elighting all as the Candy Queen
Y earning hearts with treats are so rare.

Q uitting candy is not a choice
U nder sugar sky, her realm swirls
E xquisite treats await us with delight
E ver so nice, ever so good
N ever the worst, always the best.

Mia Onwugbonu (10)
Northwood College For Girls (GDST), Northwood

Dreams

D ancing aliens, I can see running around planets
R oaring storms, I hear of the giant red planet
E xtraterrestrial beings are so mysterious I wonder
A steroids, to my surprise, go whooshing by, dodging planets skilfully
M illions of stars twinkling that dazzle me
S hiny spaceship, I fly in and out of galaxies.

Shagun Patel (9)
Northwood College For Girls (GDST), Northwood

Jungle

J aguars creeping silently through the night
U nder the sleek, majestic trees
N o one dares to step outside for death awaits the next that breathes
G orillas thud and munch and swing
L ithe snakes slither sneakily
E veryone's nightmare and everyone's hope

My jungle dream... and then I woke!

Darcey Brown (9)
Northwood College For Girls (GDST), Northwood

Dancing

D ancing the night away,
A mazing acrobats all over the place,
N ice moves you can make up,
C alm and relaxing when the time is needed,
I maginative creativity is all you need,
N eat work might need to be done,
G racious is the ballet style.

Krupali Patel (9)
Northwood College For Girls (GDST), Northwood

Billy's Dream Homework

Dreams, dreams, you think of them every night,
Even despite your height,
The morning you wake up
And the night before you go to bed,
You may even dream when you are dead.

Once upon a dream,
You can dream of blood, sweat, tears, anything really,
Maybe even when you are called Billy,
When you think of the past,
It can be any of a number of things so vast.

You can dream them in the middle of the day,
Or if you are away,
Everyone does it,
But some people a little bit.

Now we know we always dream,
They can use a rhyme scheme,
Let's say your dream is about someone dying,
Maybe that's real life
Or what your brain is saying (he may be lying).

Billy Sharples (12)
Notting Hill Preparatory School, London

A Nando's Dream

I lie in my bed and dream,
And think of a nasty scheme,
Tomorrow I shall go to Nando's,
And I'll drive there in a Lambo,
I shall use my Nando's black card,
And buy lots 'cause life is hard,
I will order mac and cheese,
And eat it in a breeze,
I will get the bottomless cup,
And fill all the way up,
A burger or a wrap,
I'll have to think ASAP,
I think I'll get the fries,
Or should I get chicken thighs?
I love the peri seasoning,
Although I'll have to get with reasoning,
Either way, it is my favourite food,
And I'll eat it all no matter the mood.

Rufus Hult (12)
Notting Hill Preparatory School, London

Dreaming

A dream,
It is such a simple thing,
It is like looking at a blank screen,
Yet can make you sing,
It is so fascinating,
How the mind works,
Sometimes it is adventure it is craving,
It is like a painter with many artworks,
A sunflower can make you dance,
And a dream can get you to the stars,
One day you'll want to prance,
And the next you'll want to fly to Mars,
They're so mysterious,
But sometimes so serious.

Electra Michalopoulou (11)
Notting Hill Preparatory School, London

I Wish I Could Be A Football Star

Football stars are my favourites,
I wish I could be one,
I can name 100,000 of them,
I wish I were one,
Ronaldo, Messi, Neymar, Mbappé,
These are my favourites of all,
They're fast and strong and kind,
I wish I could be one,
I don't mind which one,
They're all so fast and nice,
Just how I like them,
Would you want to be one?
I would, 100% for sure,
If there was something better than football,
It would be nothing but my mum,
I wish I had a cloud of wishes that could come true.

Annas Ahmadi (8)
Oakwood Junior School, Derby

Paradise!

Once in my dream, I went to a lovely island that was called Hawaii. I could see crystal-clear seas and baby turtles climbing out of the little sandpit they were hatched in. I could see lots of palm trees towering over me. I said, "I love this place. It is beautiful."
At that very moment, I felt happy and calm. My mum, dad and Sophie, my sister, all agreed with me.
We saw a dance competition and I said, "I'll have a go."
I won and even got a trophy.
Then I woke up and was getting ready for school.

Harry Astles (10)
Offley Primary Academy, Sandbach

Dream

Drinking Fiji on a sandy beach
Golden sand like in Hawaii
Kids playing in the deep blue sea
Palm tree leaves swaying above your head
Lots of people to be fed
Pens only made with fresh lead
Very nice things being said
You can't imagine the great sight
The sun shines down, it's bright light
Elated people flying their floating kites
Stare and wonder at its flight
As it reaches a tremendous height.

Jack Strain (9)
Oldbury Park Primary School, Worcester

Untitled

Every night I dream, I go zzz...
Dreams that wake me up are nightmares,
A famous wizard called Alex,
Fights dragons everywhere,
Dragons dying every day.

Powerful, famous wizards destroy dragons,
Dragons surrendering,
Wizards laughing,
Ha ha ha!
People watching the wizards fighting dragons,
Wizards winning,
While people are watching.

Kacper Aniolek (8)
Pencombe CE Primary School, Pencombe

Nightmare

Giving a miss,
To the holy words of his
The divine epitome,
Ran off from his scared arms
I lost my way back to home.
I slipped into the black deep abyss,
Caught in-between clasped hands
Of demons and devils,
Struggled hard to flee
But insanity captured me.

Mehek Iman (10)
Reddal Hill Primary School, Cradley Heath

Animals At The Zoo

A nimals live in my dreams
N arwhals have pointy horns. Splash! it went
I ce is the place for a penguin
M onkeys eat bananas, they are so funny
A nd bunnies bounce the length of a giraffe
L ittle animals have fun in the forest
S nakes slither slowly in their tank.

Harriet Dangerfield (8)
Rishworth School, Rishworth

Dreams

D reams of a beautiful Earth
R ising sun shining on the sea
E normous galaxy expanding
A nd the beautiful flowers growing
M e finding out I'm daydreaming and I'm with friends
S eeing my friends.

Gabriella Enemuwe (8)
River Mill Primary School, Dartford

Nightmares

N o, I say, this can't be,
I see this place with zombies everywhere beside me,
G athering all their brains with them,
H owever many are there, there are ten,
T ogether they march one by one,
M any of them are cooking delicious buns,
A shadow forms behind me, as quick as a flash,
R un for your lives, they say with a smash!
E rie eyes of mine were opened with a glow,
S uddenly I woke up and found out, I was in my bed, I know.

Kiana Allaraj (9)
Rydes Hill Preparatory School, Guildford

Cheeky Yoshi, My Best Friend

In my dream, I like to talk to my toys
And share all good and bad things from the day.

Yoshi is a cheeky dinosaur and Jessica is kind
My heart feels as light as a feather when I share.

We sit around the crackling fire, toasting giant, sticky marshmallows
Yoshi's marshmallow burns as hot as the sun.

Yoshi is sad, so I give him my marshmallow
Yoshi gives me a warm hug and a big, big burp.

We all have a good laugh and
I'm very happy when I am with them.

Arya Srivastava (9)
Rydes Hill Preparatory School, Guildford

Untitled

This night, when I climbed into bed, I saw the moon,
As bright as a burning fire.
Then suddenly when I fell asleep,
I saw myself falling out of an ice cream slide,
Into a land as colourful as rainbows.
Then I saw a sign saying 'Sugar Land',
What a sight I saw,
It prepared me for chocolate rivers and houses
Built of marshmallows.
But then suddenly I saw myself,
Lying in bed again.

Ajaalet Breen (9)
Rydes Hill Preparatory School, Guildford

Fantasy Land In The Sky

Every night I dream
Of a fantasy land in the sky.

Full of candyfloss clouds,
A delicious white chocolate moon
And stars made of pure gold.

I ride there on a rainbow unicorn,
Whizzing through the night sky,
Passing the birds who wave and say hello.

I feel warm and happy in this place
And want to share this with everyone.

I'm sad when I wake up
But look forward to my next sleep.

Myra Srivastava (9)
Rydes Hill Preparatory School, Guildford

Jae Speaks Two Languages

Each person comes from a different place.
Some people speak other languages,
They may sound a little strange,
But when you listen closely,
You can hear how beautiful they are.
If you ask,
You may even learn something new.
When you broaden your horizons,
Whether other languages, heritage, or culture,
You get a chance to see how much bigger the world is,
And discover how wonderful other viewpoints really are.
Even when you are the one who feels different,
You know that you have something amazing to offer the world.
You can help others to see things in new ways,
Enriching their lives with incredible warmth,
And a better understanding of who you are.
What differences do you think you have?
How can you share your special gifts with the rest of the world?

Ruth Kidane (8)
Sacred Heart Catholic Primary School, Middlesbrough

Dreaming

D reaming is easy, you just need to imagine something.
R eally dreaming is just your imagination thinking.
E ven a nightmare is dreaming but it's just a bad dream happening.
A n amazing dream is something to keep in your memory.
M ainly you should have a nice dream, a nice dream is good to have.
I n your imagination, you can do anything if you try your hardest.
N ight is when your dreams come to your imagination but nightmares happen.
G racefully embark in the world of dreams and nightmares.

Jude Weedon (9)
Sacred Heart Catholic Primary School, Middlesbrough

Superpowers

How I always wonder about having superpowers
Just so I know what's coming
To understand everything
To make the right judgement
The more I dream, it makes me want them
The more I touch, it makes me feel it
The more I scream, it makes me think it's in my heart
The more I think, it makes me think it's always with me
When danger roars with its ugly powers!

Luana Silveira (9)
St Anne's RC Primary School, Lambeth

Lucid Shadows

Monsters are pretty scary,
Not mine, his name is Lairy.
No one can see a limb,
But I can see the whole of him.
He makes me jump up and down,
Whenever he comes around.
Is it a shadow?
Am I at peace like a swallow?
While he hides in the sheets,
I've been having my treats,
On vacay.

Pema Chilanga-Halbritter (9)
St Anne's RC Primary School, Lambeth

Nightmare

N ight light's out
I see something peeping
G o to run out of bed
H ow will I survive?
T he door closes shut
M onsters crawl out
A voice calls out
R unning I go
E verything was just a nightmare.

Valentina Mora (9)
St Anne's RC Primary School, Lambeth

The Forest Melody

As I walk through the forest
Birds are singing
My sister sings with them
Making a wonderful tune
I am filled with excitement
I join in the fresh sounds
Like music, more birds join in
Our voices echo through the forest.

Armani Taffe (9)
St Anne's RC Primary School, Lambeth

My Footballing Journey

M y journey started at the park, I was freestyling with my friend
Y outh scouts for Liverpool were everywhere, including the park I was at

F or how long have I been waiting for a footballing chance? I said
"O h my goodness! he's walking over to me now." My heart was rushing
O ut of my chest. This was the best day of my life. I got signed for Liverpool
T his will be the best news my family will hear
B y tomorrow, I will be training with Liverpool
A ll of Liverpool loved me, they were so nice to me
L iverpool is my favourite football club
L aughter is everywhere
I 'm actually crying, I'm so happy, everyone is!
N o way, we won 7-0 to Man U, I scored 2 goals
G o away, Stevie G is coming towards me!

C arragher is too and Katona
A nd now I'm annoyed. Mum and Dad have to go back to Ireland
R ight now I'm going to bed. I share a room with Scholes
E veryone is ready for training but Scholes is being really annoying
E ating breakfast now
R eally, it's a dream.

Mattie McCallan (10)
St Colmcille's Primary School, Carrickmore

Benchwarmer To Hero

One day, I was playing football with my friend when a scout came over. He told us whoever scored the most goals, would be scouted.
I kicked off and got a good ball through to me. I ran through on goal but as I was about to shoot, I got slide-tackled from behind and got a free kick from 30 yards out. I shot. Goal! I scored. The scout was amazed. He called me over and said, "I want you. You're going to Man United's main team."
It was the Champions League Final and I was on the bench. It was the 90th minute. 3-3. I got subbed on. We had a last-minute corner to win it. Bruno crossed it. *Bang!* Overhead... Goal! I'd scored the winner for United. I was all over the news. I got man of the match and lifted the Champions League trophy. I became famous after that.

Ryan Loughran (10)
St Colmcille's Primary School, Carrickmore

Croke Park

C roke Park is every Irish athlete's dream
R eferee the enemy of all of the Tyrone teams
O ne puck and it's up the field
K ick the ball, see what you feel
E veryone takes part in the game

P lay with no effort, feel the shame
A cross Ireland it is not just a game
R est steady and take aim
K ick the ball, win the fame.

Eoghan Donnelly (11)
St Colmcille's Primary School, Carrickmore

Haunted House

H ow can it be that haunted?
A round the house. *Pow!*
U nder the mouldy, old, rotten house lived
N unny the Nun. She was crusty, rusty, and dusty.
T he night before, Nunny Nun rescued a little boy.
E veryone could take him away
D own in the deep woods, the nun rescued the boy

H aunted house down in the street. She took the boy
O ff and they went to the garden. A doll was
U nloved, the boy picked it up and hugged it
S o many times. He loved it so much. The
E nvious nun was so jealous of the boy

A loving lady found the boy (it was her son)
R ight away she took him home
O n the couch the boy got
U nder a blanket and had some
N ice nuggets in a bucket! How lucky
D own where Nunny Nun lived. It looked like a mansion.

Isabelle Mcleannan Greaves (9)
St Edward's CE Primary School, Castleton

High School Chaos

Normal day at high school,
Walking to class and then poof!
Long, dark corridors appear in front of me.

Scared, alone dark and misty,
I carry on walking to class,
Strangely I ended up on the basketball court.

Orange, yellow, black and grey eyes staring, hands shaking, dark figure, running, hiding.

I wake up, it's not real.
Phew!

Isabella Arrowsmith (10)
St Edward's CE Primary School, Castleton

Wizard

W izards, wizards in my dreams every night,
I always see them pass my sight,
Z ooming in others' sight with all their might,
A cross the clouds going up and down,
R ound and round in people's sight,
D own, down fast asleep.

Aizah Khan (10)
St Edward's CE Primary School, Castleton

Glitches

I love the fantasy of my dreams,
But sometimes things aren't as they seem.

Colours blue and shapes fly around,
In a world that's glitched even to the sound.

Pixels dance and sway about,
They laugh and giggle and even shout!

The glitches love to sway and swirl,
They sometimes tickle me until my toes curl!

But in these dreams where glitches shine,
I find magic from time to time.

Sometimes it's flying fish, sometimes it's not,
But it's all so fun and magical no matter what.

And finally, when my dreams come to an end,
I know that all the glitches are my friend.

Jayden Wills (9)
St Joseph's Catholic Primary School, Newbury

Weird Dreams

I always have weird dreams
Like a cloud that has steam
And one about to rain
I dream about grain
I sometimes think about rice
That has lots and lots of spice!
It is weird, right?
Just like a person in a light
Ben 10 is racist, I see
Then he gets stung by a bumblebee!
Criminals are dancing
Police glancing at them
Criminals capture the police
While the police roll the dice!
I sometimes dream of a ballet dancer
Dying from cancer!
I never dream normal dreams
I always dream weird dreams!

Ishaan Sai Prasanna (9)
St Joseph's Catholic Primary School, Newbury

We Can All Be Champions

In my gymnastics, everyone is cheering while I am doing front handsprings and cartwheels. When I do gymnastics it feels like I am living in my greatest dream. When I finish my routine everyone starts cheering louder than an erupting volcano and when they are announcing who won Champion Gymnast the crowd does a drum roll, *thud, thud, thud!*
One of the coaches announces, "And the Champion Gymnast is Melia!"
As my jaw drops, I walk up to the podium, grab my award and bow and everyone is cheering louder than ever.

Melia Payne (9)
St Mary's Catholic Primary School, Canton

Games!

Step inside my colourful dream where it's imaginary
It's going to be fun!
Now I want to show you my home
Welcome!
Now what do you see?
What do you feel?
I feel as joyful as a happy tree
Dance with the wind because you're here!
Now what do you think of my PS4 and 5?
It's so cool to me.
Click! Clack! Click!
Oh no! The lights turned off!
Don't be scared
We could go outside
But we need to find the door
Oh no!
I can't find the door
Now we are really stuck!
Argh!
Ting!

Phew! It was a dream
Now I can go back to sleep
Without warning
Click!

Naomi Solomon (9)
St Mary's Catholic Primary School, Canton

The Mansion

I dreamt of... a beautiful mansion that was made out of strong metal. It was shiny. The mansion was empty downstairs. I went upstairs, it was full of cotton candy. It looked as delicious as caramel popcorn. I could see a chocolate bar on a shiny table - *crunch!* There was a PS5 in a room. I picked up the amazing controller. The PS5 was so fashionable.

I wished I could stay there forever and play FC 24 and victory 2-1! The gamers were giggling as they went on and on. I saw a party room. I had so much fun.

Joel Eze (9)
St Mary's Catholic Primary School, Canton

A Dream I Have Had Before

Oh, I had a dream
I dreamed of going to school
Where my teacher eats doughnuts
My friends bring pets such as unicorns

Oh, I had a dream
I dreamt that I was in the noisy forest
With fairies dancing
Butterflies bouncing
Cheetahs chattering
Birds singing
Waterfalls *swishy swashy!*

Oh, I had a dream
I dreamed that I was a dark cavegirl
Where I painted a picture of mammoths
Clouds and people.

Jessica Gerrie (8)
St Matthew's Church Of England Primary School, Redhill

Unicorn Dreams

Have you heard about my magical dream?
It was full of unicorns eating cotton candy.
It was a beautiful place.
Gummy bears walked by drinking Coke.
Then a white bunny hopped by.
It was holding a jar of sticky, gooey honey.
In the sky, I spied a majestic castle.
I flew up to the castle door.
A princess appeared and said hello.
She gave me a smile and gave me a treat.
Then I heard my alarm beat.

Gracielle Romero (7)
St Matthew's Church Of England Primary School, Redhill

The Creepy Clowns

Creepy clowns are chasing

   C reepy clowns are terrifying monsters
   R unning in the creepy house
   E nchanting for people to be found
   E ach person doesn't dare to go inside
   P ouncing for someone to go inside
   Y oung children are very scared

   C lowns fight for lives
   L ives are very strong
   O thers are very weak
  W eakness makes it harder
   N othing will stop the clowns from attacking
   S urprisingly, it doesn't exist nowadays.

Richard Buzenschi (10)
St Meryl School, Watford

The Fairies That Live

F ar, far away, fairies live
A fter a year, they all die, but one
I 'm so sad, they all die but me, why? Why?
R eally, across town, another fairy lived
I said, "They all died but me, why? Why?"
E very year, they cried
S oon, after three years, they met in the town, bumped into each other, they were looking for food. They jumped with joy and they lived happily ever after.

Indi Horwood (10)
St Meryl School, Watford

The Good Dream

There was a little boy who wanted to be living on the stars and the moon, so in his dreams, all he could see was stars, magic and the moon. It was the best dream of his and he could do special tricks when he drank his homemade drink. He could do more and make magic and could make more to bring other children and bring their wishes true. When he awoke, he told his family the good news and things were normal.

Louis F (10)
St Meryl School, Watford

My Dream Horse

I dreamt about
a bay, beautiful horse
with a furry coat
and a lovely sense of humour.
A soft-like-pillow tail,
two magical sparkling eyes.
Crunch, crunch on hay or grass,
clip-clop in the fields,
nothing but sun for new dreams.

Ruth Prelipcean (10)
St Meryl School, Watford

These Are My Dreams For The Future

I want to be the first child to own a pet on the moon,
And meet a baboon that has been to the planets,
And help change it back to an alien baboon,
My dreams for the future.

I want to meet dogs, cats, rabbits and bats,
Help them all before they fall down the hole
Like a mole
And meet their end,
These are my dreams for the future.

I make everyone alright after they are bad,
And help them to play around all day,
Have fun in the smiling sun and have lots of fun,
My dreams for the future.

I also want to go to the mad moon
And meet the alien baboon,
And be with my friends I have
Met over the years on the mad moon,
My dreams for the future.

And escalate from Earth to the moon,
In a rocket ship that is so blue,
It stands out on the moon
My dreams for the future

I was as happy as could ever be,
But everything went dark,
Thunder roared in the distance
My dreams ended,
My dreams for the future.

Esmay Bou-Yeldham
St Michael's CE Primary School, Braintree

Longing For Summer

Lately, it seems like all the time, I look out the window, and all I see is rain and dark clouds, which show many frowns.
I long for the sunny days and all the plays – the splashing, dashing and laughing with family and friends.
When will I see a bright blue sky and sunshine on me and mine while we dine?
I have that feeling of excitement knowing the summer is coming and soon my feet will be on the ground at the beach without a frown beside my hound.
Here's to summertime, rhymes and fun times.

Charlotte Dixon (10)
St Patrick's Catholic Primary School, Leeds

Imagination

Welcome to a world of your imagination
Where everything is your creation
You can bring all your fascination to life
Just take my hand and we will begin, with a spin and follow the wind
Come, gather around and you'll see a nation come together and just remember it is a dream that you have seen.

Adaeze Anyawueze (10)
St Patrick's Catholic Primary School, Leeds

Superpowers

S pider-Man, Superman and Batman!
U niverse is saved again!
P eople clap and cheer!
E nemies are defeated once again!
R unning around the city is hard work!
P lanet Earth has been saved once more!
O nly villains will not win!
W e will fight to the end!
E ven villains are not the best!
R ule superheroes to the very end!
S uperheroes! Superheroes! Go! Go! Go!

Hasnain Bhatia (8)
St Pius X Catholic Preparatory School, Fulwood

The Football Match In Space

There was a footballer who came out on the field. He was happy. Winner's prize was a trip to Space Chickens. In a rocket and cold spocket. In a rocket they were in space and they saw Space Chicken with colourful feathers. They came down to Earth and they ate food and lived happily.

Tinaye Mleng (9)
St Pius X Catholic Preparatory School, Fulwood

Fluttering Dreams

In the sun's embrace, delightful flower fairies dance,
Their wings a-twinkle, shoes a-glitter,
Among them I stand, in a trance.
I look left and right but all I see,
Each one, unfurling a fragrant bloom.

Intrigued, I reach out to touch a delicate petal,
But like a dream, they drift away on a whispering breeze.
Gasping, I watch their flight with glee,
As they twirl away, wild and free.

Surrounded, I close my eyes,
A soft caress upon my cheek,
Awakening at home, to my surprise,
Beneath my pillow, "A fairy wand!" I squeak.

Hana Swain (9)
Stanborough Primary School, Garston

Ghost Roam

G host roam...
H unted by the human creatures...
O h no! Here they come! Quick, hide!
S o, so miserable...
T hese human creatures...

R ight! I want to escape!
O h, I can slide through these walls!
A t last, I'm free!
M ay I ask what you're doing? (Ghost: "Ugh, no!")

Fatima Moshen (8)
Stanborough Primary School, Garston

Footballer

In my dreams
Fitness is an award
An outcome
Of my discovery
Inspired by friendships
The goal to be my best
Out on the football field
The kindness of breathing
Running, kicking
Watching the sport unravel
before me
This must be for me
My valid joy
Football.

Ved Patel (9)
Stanborough Primary School, Garston

Untitled

Once upon a time, in a land of dreams,
I sailed the seas on a pirate ship, or so it seemed,
With Peter Pan by my side, we flew high and free,
Through the starry skies, just him, the ship and me.

The Jolly Roger fluttered, the waves crashed below,
Adventure beckoned, where we'd go, we didn't know.
Mermaids sang sweetly, their voices carried on the wind,
Telling tales of treasures, of adventures to rescind.

Alexander Wilson-Reeves (8)
Sutterton Fourfields CE Primary School, Sutterton

The Helping Hand

I am not magic
But I am fantastic
I am not hurtful
But I am helpful
I am not selfish
But I am kind, caring and beautiful.

Mollie Quincey (8)
Sutterton Fourfields CE Primary School, Sutterton

A Space Walk

Going to a massive, white rocket,
Going to the moon in a white, orange jacket,
Off we go into space,
We're in space, it is dark and black,
We're in the galaxy and I am having a look!

I am on the moon, bang! The rocket landed,
I am on the moon, my life was almost ended,
I am nervous,
I can see something,
It is a little green alien.

We start to see more,
We start to run,
Slowly, they get faster,
We get to the rocket,
Suddenly, my mum woke me up.

Sebastian Williams (10)
The King's School, Gloucester

Flying Over Meteors

Horses are fun and beautiful,
They go on adventures and jump meteors,
So if you've had a bad day, go and ride them.

Today is the big day,
The day of the show,
There are winners and losers.

We have arrived and we're doing Chase Me, Charlie,
I warm him up and now it's my time to go in,
He jumps and it feels like we're flying,
And the crowd roars like a lion.

Pippa Hay (10)
The King's School, Gloucester

Where The Fairies Fly

It was dark and the sky was black,
In my dream there were fairies,
Fluttering above the sky,
Swooping and flying up high into,
The sky went all the fairies,
Sprinkling fairy dust onto me,
Then another fairy started pointing to,
A colourful house, in went all the,
Fairies to dance all the night,
And they started to party, in my dream,
Went the fairies swooping against,
Me to make me fall asleep then,
One by one they made a tower,
To make me fall asleep they jumped one,
By one to have fun and make me,
Dream about where the fairies,
Fly in a magical mist then again,
They took turns to make me look,
At them, then after midnight,
I fell asleep and dreamt about,
Where the fairies fly.

Lima Sadyar (8)
The Oval Primary School, Birmingham

Bedtime Dreams

One time, in my dreams, I saw a very scary dream. In my dream I saw that a girl was laughing and it was in the middle of a mountain. I was selling food and they pushed me down on the floor. Then I shouted in my dream and my own tummy was shaking. That time I felt so scared.

I had a very exciting dream. Once upon a time, I had a very happy dream. When I was in a dream, I saw a fairy and the fairy's voice was beautiful. Then she asked me, "Do you want to fly?"

I said very fast, "Yes, I want to fly." Then I put my feet on the ground and I saw a beautiful garden and there were many fairies and that dream was my favourite dream ever.

Lubna Hatif (8)
The Oval Primary School, Birmingham

Scary Nightmare

Once, I went to sleep. Then I had a dream but that dream wasn't a dream, it was a nightmare. So, on my birthday, I was at a fair and a man came up to me and said, "This is a nightmare, so don't be scared."
Me and my family rushed home but left me home alone. I was all terrified, the same man from earlier stalked me home. He said, "Don't be scared, because this is still a nightmare!"
As fast as a flash, I rushed upstairs. I was so scared I looked out my window. Someone was dead. I was looking for my phone but it was in the car and my family went far, far away... I heard they went to the other side of England.

Binyamin Shah (9)
The Oval Primary School, Birmingham

Getting Lost In The Middle Of The Dark

In the middle of the dark a tiny shadow appeared out of nowhere. Nothing but me was there. I was terrified, the shadow kept on moving. *What could it be?* I asked myself. Could it be an animal, person, a monster? I didn't know. My friends were out there looking for food. I didn't know what to do. I tried calling my friends' names but they couldn't hear me. I thought it was one of my friends but it wasn't.
I was lost. I didn't know where to go, only my friends knew, because they'd brought me here. All I could see was darkness and trees. I was starving. When were my friends gonna come? What if they got lost?

Fatima Latif (9)
The Oval Primary School, Birmingham

The Lost One

There I was standing in the cold mist,
Thinking of all the ones I missed,
The sky was the only thing to be seen,
It got me confused as to why it was green,
Not even one bit of sunshine was there,
I couldn't bear it,
All my nightmares came to life,
There he was holding a knife,
His crazy hair,
Looked like a fair,
His knife was covered in blood,
It made my heart thud,
His crazy smile made me shiver,
His pockets were full of silver,
Then there was my last scream.

Anayah Bibi (9)
The Oval Primary School, Birmingham

Lost Under The Sea

I have to practise for a swimming competition,
Mum, I am going to practice okay bye-bye,
See you, Lea get in the water let's do this,
Come on, oh no why are you drowning,
No, no, no, I am a mess there,
But I am running out of breath, argh,
No no no, I am running out of breath!
No, no, ow why,
Is my head red blood, no no!
I am drowning oh no! Why am I in the house?
Oh sweetie you are okay,
No, my head hurt, no no my girl,
She is diving.

Maya Anasiasta (9)
The Oval Primary School, Birmingham

At The End Of The Rainbow

I have been looking for the end of the rainbow and now I have finally found it.

There are unicorns with rainbow manes and they are on wings, and there are really cool swings at the end of the rainbow, there are gold coins and the unicorns' horns are shiny silver at the end of the rainbow.

Fairies fly high and they reach towards the sky, there's soft fluffy clouds and I'm proud that I found the end of the rainbow.

Aila Hussain (8)
The Oval Primary School, Birmingham

The Little Boy With A Wizard

I was in a scary place, where no one was there,
Only me and a creepy wizard.
I was scared that he would turn me into a frog,
Because he had a magical stick,
Although he got that stick from a witch.
He was so big, even ten elephants,
Were as tall as him.
He could turn into everything,
There was nothing he couldn't turn into.
He was a strong, huge, big wizard,
And he was the biggest in the world.

Mohammed Hassan (9)
The Oval Primary School, Birmingham

Gymnastics

G et up and do your flips before you do your tricks
Y et again, go and get blamed before you get trained
M ythical dragon, go and get a gymnastic dragon
N ow you witch, go and get a stitch
A crobatic leadership
S weat falling on the floor like rain dripping to the step
T he end, we finally get an ice cream.

Umaima Asim (8)
The Oval Primary School, Birmingham

A Princess On Ice

Every night, Peach saw a sight of ice,
She wanted to be a skater and she was, a moment later.
No trips, only amazing jumps and skips,
Everyone threw flowers for hours.
A girl called Cherry threw a berry,
But Peach didn't trip, she did an amazing flip,
Even though everyone else wanted her to slip.

Aiza Hussain (8)
The Oval Primary School, Birmingham

Lost At Sea

I was lost at sea, and I had to wee.
With Karen as captain, I was being pampered by a bee.
I looked around at the sea.
What I could see was that I still had to wee,
But I was being pampered by a bee.
It was too late.
Ten minutes later, I walked the plank.
I survived because of a clown mermaid.

Aisha Ali (9)
The Oval Primary School, Birmingham

Royalty

The palace was full of guests,
So I got ready and acted my best,
My jewellery was made of gold,
The Queen was graceful and bold,
The carriage had wheels of silver,
As watched the gemstone glimmer,
I crouched down to get my crown,
And in the crowd, there was not a single frown.

Safiyyah Islam (9)
The Oval Primary School, Birmingham

Dragons

As the smoke curled around me, I felt like I was choking. Hot, fiery breath was talking to me.
As the dragon landed, I thought he was going to eat me, but he didn't. He would allow me to ride on his back. So off we went.
But then I fell in the ocean and the dragon came to save me.

Muhammad Zubair (9)
The Oval Primary School, Birmingham

Power

To some, power is guns,
To some, power is knives,
To some, power is the ability to read and write,
To some, power is control,
To some, power is first,
To some, like Dr Martin Luther King Jr, power was words,
To some, power is like a trapped animal, trying to get out,
To some, power is love,
To some, power is art,
To some, power is money,
To me power is knowledge,
So what is power to you?

Tianna-Mai Jones (10)
The Ridgeway Primary School, Reading

Up In The Clouds

I saw rainbows in the air
Coming to my eyes with flare.
I saw Rebeca wanting me to come in the sky.
I was overjoyed, I got carried on Rebeca and it
was one, two, three, up in the air!
I felt like I was on a jet, relaxing in a chair.
Rebeca went as high as giraffe, but I realised she
wanted to talk to me about something,
She had a baby, I was elated with joy.
My heart was booming,
But three little fairies wanted us
And led us
On a football pitch, I was with Saka
With Rebeca
On my side.
She left to give birth, I had no one on my side
I was lonely, I wondered what was going to
happen next
I just needed help...
He was not Saka, he was a stranger waiting for me to
have a chat with him
But I couldn't trust him.

He wasn't anyone I know, I went in Minecraft, having to complete an obby,
What was going to happen next?

Janiah Katenda (7)
Towers Junior School, Hornchurch

My Horrific Dream

In the night I had a horrific dream,
Dark, fiery, ghostly and mean,
I woke up with a menacing scream,
Just because of that stupid scene.

The vampire's hands held me tight,
But if I screamed with fright,
It said it would haunt me in the night,
Then, someone stopped it with all of their might.

It was my amazing friend coming to save me,
I just had to think of me being free,
So that I could wake up from my horrific dream.

Kyra Sains (10)
Towers Junior School, Hornchurch

Booming Business

When I close my eyes, I dream...
My future is clear to me.
The success I achieve
Is plain to see
Black business suit I wear.
My aspirations I want to share.

When I close my eyes, I dream...
An office high in the sky.
Plenty of space for my dreams to fly.

When I close my eyes and dream
I know my future will be
A chance to achieve the best for me.

George Rayner (11)
Towers Junior School, Hornchurch

Football!

Football is my best friend.
A friend who I play with twenty-four-seven.
I miss it when I don't play.
It's illegal.
Football makes me feel fit, healthy and strong, with lots and lots of energy.
"Heads up!" I pass to him.
I always play well with my energy.
I can't wait until my football match next weekend, so I can shoot, pass and everything.
I will destroy them ten-nil.

Cassius Castro (9)
Trawden Forest Primary School, Trawden

Disneyland

Disneyland is one of the best lands ever,
I'll just tell you now, you'll like the weather.
Because I'm sure you all like spring,
And I think you all like to sing as well.

So now I will invite you to Disneyland,
So you can play in the sand.
We will get on the Polar Express,
And when we get there, we'll scream, "Yes!"

When we wake there, we will go to a flat
And buy a dog that will sleep on a mat.

Isla Rossiter (9)
Wembdon St George's CE VC Primary School, Wembdon

Spring

S ummer is here
P eople are happy
R abbits are hopping along in the grass
I n the air, birds are singing
N ew lambs are arriving
G oing out for long warm walks.

Indie Rogers (10)
Wembdon St George's CE VC Primary School, Wembdon

The Amazing Journey Of Food

When the lights turn off, I close my eyes,
In a land full of food, this is what's inside,
I see sushi as a football, I quickly score a goal,
On my way somewhere else, there's Meatball as a foal.

I hear buzzing chicken nuggets,
They're as small as a petal,
Then suddenly, the clanging of a bucket,
As it hits something metal.

I smell icing and sugar being poured on a doughnut,
I have an allergy, so I hope there are no nuts,
There's flopping flower fish on the floor,
And they're as stinky as a dinosaur.

I feel my head bumping into a gingerbread house,
Looking up, I see it's the shape of a mouse,
With jelly beans all over,
Inside lies a cake, the shape of a clover.

After eating the cake, I awake,
With a frown on my face,
I miss that magical place.

Sofia Ishaq (9)
Whetstone Field Primary School, Walsall

Living Underwater

We are underwater and look over there,
The fish are as happy as can be,
The octopus is waving his tentacles everywhere,
Underwater, everyone is full of glee.

Oh no, don't go over there,
I warn you,
The sharks are as scary as a grizzly bear!
In the night, you can hear them,
Chasing their prey,
If an animal goes over there,
They won't see another day.

Meet the mermaids,
They're so pretty, can't you see?
Let's go over there,
Look, they're inviting us for a cup of tea.

The mermaids are making a fresh pie,
Over at their sparkling cottage,
I really want some,
I can't lie.

Ivy Wilkes (9)
Whetstone Field Primary School, Walsall

Sealand

In Sealand, you're in the sea,
There are hills, meadows and towers in the distance,
In the sea there's more than you can conceive,
The seas will make you smile and go to the reefs.

You can hear the fish, the coral and the water,
With coral swaying, it's as peaceful as space,
So close your eyes and the fish swim beside you,
Go on, it's only you and me here.

If you try, you will smell a lovely scent,
If you try, you will hear gushing and whooshing,
If you try, you will see passion and glory,
If you try, you will not feel any guilt or be gory.

Pratik Shah (8)
Whetstone Field Primary School, Walsall

Wonderland

The day is over and I'm getting into bed,
I close my eyes and wonder where my imagination will take me,
And there I am, in a world of dreams,
Where candyfloss twirls,
And ice cream chatters,
And then I feel something pushing against my leg.

And then I look down,
I see a ginger cat,
With stripes like a tiger,
And teeth like a lion.

Then we go on a roller coaster,
With corndog in my molar,
My cat jumps on my lap, with a cute little peep,
And jumps on my feet.

Fearne Karim (9)
Whetstone Field Primary School, Walsall

Once Upon A Dog Dream

You can see blue blossom in a dog dream
With cats in the tree meowing with glee
You see dogs bathing in the river
And the river is as clear as can be.

You can smell beautiful pink tulips
With the smell of minty air
The grass is as green as dazzling green emeralds
With cats smelling like a dream.

You feel the wind blowing through your hair
You can feel blue blossom swaying about
You look and see dogs coming to hug, but be aware
They might nibble your hair.

Freddy Montgomery (8)
Whetstone Field Primary School, Walsall

Upside-Down Dreamland

It is Upside-Down Dreamland,
The sky is as blue as a sky,
The floor is covered in clouds
And the birds have pretty pink feet.

The pretty pink blossom
Scattered on the ground
While the roots of the trunk
Scattered underneath the tall canopy.

Above our heads
Water got our beds,
It splashed,
Black and angry,
Splashed the water
Like catching its prey.
Whoosh goes the wings longer than a boat sail.

Ollie Whiting (9)
Whetstone Field Primary School, Walsall

YOUNG WRITERS INFORMATION

We hope you have enjoyed reading this book – and that you will continue to in the coming years.

If you're a young writer who enjoys reading and creative writing, or the parent of an enthusiastic poet or story writer, do visit our website www.youngwriters.co.uk. Here you will find free competitions, workshops and games, as well as recommended reads, a poetry glossary and our blog.

If you would like to order further copies of this book, or any of our other titles, then please give us a call or visit www.youngwriters.co.uk.

Young Writers
Remus House
Coltsfoot Drive
Peterborough
PE2 9BF
(01733) 890066
info@youngwriters.co.uk

YoungWritersUK YoungWritersCW
youngwriterscw youngwriterscw